W9-AOP-068

FLORIDA
MARLINS

by Bo Smolka

Published by ABDO Publishing Company, 8000 West 78th Street, Edina, Minnesota 55439. Copyright © 2011 by Abdo Consulting Group, Inc. International copyrights reserved in all countries. No part of this book may be reproduced in any form without written permission from the publisher. SportsZone™ is a trademark and logo of ABDO Publishing Company.

Printed in the United States of America,
North Mankato, Minnesota
112010
012011

Editor: Matt Tustison
Copy Editor: Nicholas Cafarelli
Interior Design and Production: Kazuko Collins
Cover Design: Christa Schneider

Photo Credits: H. Rumph Jr./AP Images, cover; Kathy Willens/AP Images, 1; Elise Amendola/AP Images, 4, 42 (middle); Eric Draper/AP Images, 7; Hans Deryk/AP Images, 8, 20, 42 (bottom); Ed Reinke/AP Images, 11; Jennie Zeiner/AP Images, 12; Doug Jennings/AP Images, 15, 42 (top); Lynne Sladky/AP Images, 17, 34, 43 (bottom); Jeffrey Boan/AP Images, 19; Gary I. Rothstein/AP Images, 22; Michael S. Green/AP Images, 25; Bill Kostroun/AP Images, 26, 43 (middle); Wilfredo Lee/AP Images, 29; J. Pat Carter/AP Images, 30, 43 (top); Charles Krupa/AP Images, 33; David Zalubowski/AP Images, 36; Alan Diaz/AP Images, 39; The Miami Herald, Marice Cohn Band/AP Images, 40; Ed Betz/AP Images, 44; Julia Roberton/AP Images, 47

Library of Congress Cataloging-in-Publication Data
Smolka, Bo, 1965-
  Florida Marlins / by Bo Smolka.
    p. cm. — (Inside MLB)
  ISBN 978-1-61714-044-0
  1. Florida Marlins (Baseball team—History—Juvenile literature. I. Title.
  GV875.F56S66 2011
  796.357'6409759381—dc22
                            2010036563

TABLE OF CONTENTS

CHAPTER 1

CHAMPIONS!

he Florida Marlins' Edgar Renteria stood at home plate, his bat twitching as he awaited the pitch. Craig Counsell took his lead off third base. He represented the winning run, 90 feet away. The bases were loaded. The crowd was going wild.

This was not just any game. It was Game 7 of the 1997 World Series. It was the bottom of the 11th inning. For just the third time, Game 7 of the World Series had gone into extra innings.

The Marlins had trailed the Cleveland Indians 2–1 going into the bottom of the ninth but tied the score on a sacrifice fly

Extra! Extra!

The World Series is a best-of-seven series. It has been held nearly every year since 1903. But, through 2009, Game 7 had gone into extra innings only three times. Florida's win over Cleveland in 1997 was one of them. The others occurred in 1924, when the Washington Senators defeated the New York Giants 4–3 in 12 innings, and in 1991, when the Minnesota Twins beat the Atlanta Braves 1–0 in 10 innings.

The Marlins' Edgar Renteria is hoisted by teammates after he hit a game-winning single in Game 7 of the 1997 World Series.

by Counsell, Florida's second baseman.

Now it was the 11th inning and Renteria, the team's shortstop, was batting with two outs. Indians pitcher Charles Nagy fired home to Renteria. A big curveball dropped over the plate. Strike one. On Nagy's next pitch, Renteria sliced a line drive back up the middle and into center field. Base hit! Counsell sprinted down the third-base line, stomped on home plate, and leaped into the arms of teammates.

In just their fifth season, the Marlins were World Series champions.

"It [doesn't] get any better than this; it can't get any better than this," outfielder Jeff Conine said. "We're the world champions!"

It was a scene few could have imagined even a few weeks earlier. The Marlins had not even won their division. They finished the regular season with a record of 92–70, their best ever, but the team finished nine games behind the powerhouse Atlanta Braves in the National League (NL) East. Florida, though, made the playoffs as a wild-card team.

Some franchises build their teams by developing young players in the minor leagues. The Marlins built their 1997 team with owner Wayne Huizenga's money. He paid several of the best free agents millions of dollars to play for the Marlins.

Just days after the 1996 season ended, the Marlins hired Jim Leyland as their manager. He had led the Pittsburgh Pirates to three straight division titles from 1990 to 1992.

Then, in November 1996, the Marlins began their spending spree on players when they signed power-hitting third

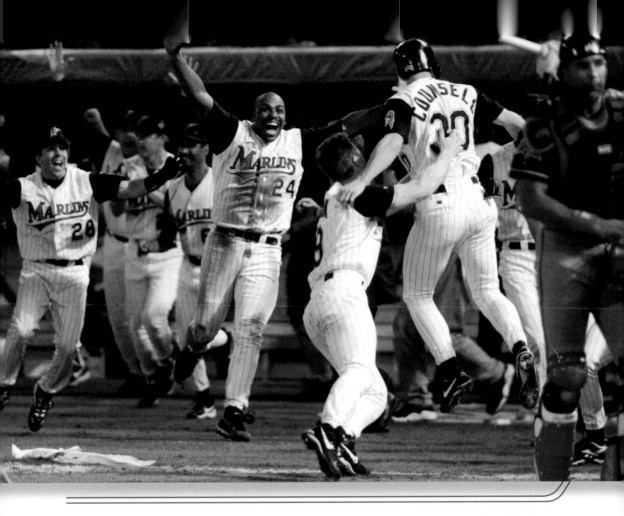

Craig Counsell leaps after scoring the title-clinching run in the 1997 World Series. Teammates, including Bobby Bonilla (24), celebrate with him.

baseman Bobby Bonilla. He had been a four-time All-Star while playing for Leyland in Pittsburgh. Florida went on to sign All-Star outfielder Moises Alou, a former Montreal Expo, and ex-Chicago White Sox ace pitcher Alex Fernandez.

The Marlins, who had never had a winning season, suddenly found themselves challenging for a playoff spot. They reached the All-Star break in 1997 with a record of 50–36.

They could not catch the Braves in the NL East, but they

All-Star outfielder Moises Alou was one of the key players the free-spending Marlins added before the 1997 season.

did not need to. With a 6–3 win at Montreal on September 23, Florida clinched the NL wild-card spot.

The Marlins were in the playoffs.

Florida had its off-season shopping spree to thank. Alou led the team with 23 home runs and 115 runs batted in (RBIs).

Bonilla hit .297 with 96 RBIs. Fernandez led the team in wins with 17.

The Marlins opened the playoffs against the San Francisco Giants in the NL Division Series (NLDS). Florida quickly showed its playoff magic. The Marlins won the first two games with singles in the bottom of the ninth inning. They finished off the Giants in Game 3 of the best-of-five series with a 6–2 road victory.

That earned the Marlins a spot in the best-of-seven NL Championship Series (NLCS) against the mighty Braves. Atlanta finished the 1997 regular season with a major league-best 101–61 record. The Braves had won four of the past five NL pennants.

The Marlins set the tone early in the NLCS, however, scoring three runs in the top of the first inning of Game 1. They won 5–3 that night behind starting pitcher Kevin Brown. The Braves fought back. After four games, the series was tied at two wins apiece. In Game 5, Florida started 22-year-old rookie pitcher Livan Hernandez against Atlanta ace Greg Maddux, who had gone 19–4 in the regular season. Maddux

WILD CARDS

Major League Baseball (MLB) was set to introduce the wild card in 1994, after the two leagues reorganized into three divisions each. Before then, the American League (AL) and the NL each had two divisions. The division champions met in the league championship series, and the winners of those series squared off in the World Series.

After switching to three divisions, baseball had a problem: How can three teams have a playoff? The solution was the wild card.

Beginning in 1995 (there were no playoffs in 1994 because of a strike), the second-place team with the best record in each league also made the playoffs. That is how the 1997 Marlins qualified. They became the first wild-card team to win the World Series. Florida captured the title as a wild card again in 2003. The 2002 Los Angeles Angels and the 2004 Boston Red Sox also won the World Series as wild cards.

was good, allowing just two runs in seven innings. Hernandez was even better. He threw a complete game, giving up one run on three hits. He struck out 15, a league championship series record, and the host Marlins won 2–1.

Two days later in Atlanta, the Marlins prevailed 7–4 in Game 6 to win the pennant. Florida, a wild-card team, was going to the World Series.

The Marlins faced the Indians in the Series. At times, neither team looked as if it deserved to be the champion. Pitchers struggled to throw strikes. In Game 3, the teams combined for six errors. Game 4 was played in record cold in frigid Cleveland. The game-time temperature was 38 degrees. Snow showers fell during batting practice. But after winning 8–7 in Game 5, the Marlins returned to Florida with a three-games-to-two lead in the Series. They only needed one more victory.

The Indians denied them in Game 6, with Chad Ogea outpitching Brown in a 4–1 Cleveland win. That set up the dramatic Game 7.

The Most Valuable Player (MVP) of the World Series was not one of the Marlins' big free-agent signings. It was Hernandez. He became the first rookie pitcher in 50 years to win two World Series starts. He won Game 1 and Game 5. Behind Hernandez and the high-priced stars, surprising Florida ruled the baseball universe.

The reign, though, did not last long.

The Marlins' Livan Hernandez delivers a pitch during Game 5 of the 1997 World Series. The rookie played like a veteran in the postseason that year.

CHAPTER 2

MORE THAN SPRING TRAINING

*C*onsidering that Florida is known as the "Sunshine State," it might seem strange that no big-league baseball team called Florida home before 1993.

There is plenty of good baseball in the state. The University of Miami is a college powerhouse. Through 2010, it had won four national championships. Furthermore, many major league teams hold spring training in Florida. As they prepare for the season in February and March, the players like the warm sunshine that Florida provides.

The weather, ironically, was always viewed as a reason that Florida did not have a major league team. Summers in South Florida can be rainy, muggy, and miserable. There was another major hurdle: There was no true big-league ballpark in which a Florida team could play.

In 1990, the NL announced that it would expand, adding

Marlins owner Wayne Huizenga, shown in 1997, was responsible for getting a big-league team for the Miami, Florida, area in the early 1990s.

two teams. Wayne Huizenga, a multimillionaire who was already part-owner of the Miami Dolphins pro football team, made a strong case for South Florida to get an MLB team. He had a solution to the stadium problem: Huizenga was also part-owner of Joe Robbie Stadium, in which the Dolphins played. Huizenga said the football stadium could be reconfigured for baseball. Huizenga's long-term goal was to have a ballpark built for the baseball team. For the time being, though, he said the football stadium would suffice.

Huizenga's plan worked. He beat out two other Florida candidates—Orlando and Tampa-St. Petersburg—along with Buffalo, New York, and Washington DC. On July 5, 1991, major league owners approved the Florida Marlins and the Colorado Rockies as expansion teams to begin play in 1993.

"What a tremendous day this is for Florida," Huizenga said. "Today, history was made."

Even though the team was based in Miami in the state's southeast tip, Huizenga called it the Florida Marlins. He wanted fans throughout the state to feel like the team was theirs.

A marlin is a large saltwater game fish. Huizenga, who liked sportfishing, named the team the Marlins because he considered the marlin to be a fierce fighter.

Florida finally had a team, a name, and, at least temporarily, a stadium. Now it needed to find players. That job fell primarily to the team's first general manager, Dave Dombrowski.

In June each year, baseball holds its amateur draft.

Catcher Charles Johnson, the Marlins' first draft pick ever, holds up a Florida jersey after signing with the team in November 1992.

Through this draft, major league teams select the top high school and college players.

In 1992, for the first time, Florida took part in the draft. With their first pick, the Marlins chose catcher Charles Johnson, who had been a star at the University of Miami.

Glovin' It

The Marlins made Charles Johnson their first draft pick ever. He made them look very smart. From 1995 to 1998, Johnson won four straight Gold Glove Awards. That award is given each season to the best defensive player at each position. In 1997, Johnson set a major league record for a catcher by handling 973 chances without an error.

players went on strike. They refused to play as they and the owners bickered over money and other issues. For the first time in 90 years, the World Series was not held.

When the strike was finally settled in 1995, many former baseball fans refused to go to games. Doing so would mean that they were supporting greedy players and owners, they believed. Overall, baseball attendance dropped by 20 percent in 1995. The Marlins'

attendance fell by more than 36 percent between 1993 and 1995.

On the field, Florida's struggles continued. The Marlins finished the shortened 1994 season 51–64. The 1995 season began late, after the strike was resolved in April, and Florida finished 67–76. Conine remained one of the bright spots. He led the Marlins with 25 home runs and 105 RBIs.

With the team in the midst of a seven-game losing streak in July 1996, manager Rene Lachemann was fired. John Boles, who worked in the team's front office, took over as manager. Florida finished 80–82, its best record to that point.

Still, through four seasons, the Marlins had enjoyed little success on the field. Attendance was lagging. Something needed to be done.

Closing Time

Relief pitcher Bryan Harvey was Florida's closer in 1993. He finished with 45 saves and made the NL All-Star team. Also a member of the 1993 Marlins, though, was the player who would become baseball's all-time saves leader. Trevor Hoffman was picked by the Marlins in the 1992 expansion draft and went 2–2 with two saves for Florida in 1993. Midway through that season, he was traded to the San Diego Padres for Gary Sheffield.

Jeff Conine, shown in 1997, emerged as a steady player for Florida during the team's first several seasons.

That led Huizenga to hire former Pittsburgh manager Jim Leyland as Florida's manager and to go after high-priced free agents. In the fall of 1996, Huizenga let his money do the talking, and the message was loud and clear: We want to win now.

CHAPTER 3

FROM FIRST
TO WORST

On the field, things were looking up in 1997. Led by all their free-agent acquisitions, the Marlins were winning. Off the field, trouble was brewing.

Owner Wayne Huizenga, who had spent so freely in the off-season, said he was losing millions of dollars on the team. The baseball-only stadium he wanted built for his team did not yet exist. Attendance was down. For a variety of reasons—the strike, a poor stadium for baseball, the losing seasons—fans had lost interest. So Huizenga announced in June 1997 that the Marlins were for sale.

Luis Castillo

Second baseman Luis Castillo was signed by Florida in 1992 in his native Dominican Republic, just before he turned 17 years old. He reached the major leagues by age 20. He was on the Marlins' World Series teams of 1997 and 2003, and he also endured the 108-loss season of 1998. In 2002, Castillo had a 35-game hitting streak. He was traded after the 2005 season to the Minnesota Twins. Through 2010, he still held the record for most games as a Marlin with 1,128.

Empty seats at the Marlins' home stadium became a common sight in 1998 after the team traded away many of its best players.

Shown in November 1997, Wayne Huizenga discusses his efforts to sell the Marlins. He said he was losing millions of dollars owning the team.

He said that to be successful, the Marlins needed a new baseball stadium. He wanted the government to help pay for it. But a lot of people in Florida did not think that the government should pay for a millionaire's ballpark.

Huizenga knew that any new owner probably could not afford to lose as much money as he had lost on the team. The quickest way to cut costs was to cut the big salaries. So less than a month after their World Series win, the Marlins began trading many of their top players, usually for cheap minor leaguers. It became known as a fire sale.

Moises Alou, who led the 1997 Marlins with 23 home runs and 115 RBIs? Gone. He was traded to the Houston Astros for three minor leaguers. Ace pitcher Kevin Brown, who went 16–8 in 1997? Gone, traded to the San Diego Padres for minor leaguers.

The shakeup spared no one. Even Jeff Conine, "Mr. Marlin," was traded to the Kansas City Royals.

By Opening Day of 1998, nearly half of the players from the Marlins' World Series team were gone. In their places were a lot of rookies and minor leaguers. The result was disastrous. The Marlins went from first to worst.

One year after winning the World Series, the Marlins lost 108 games. After the season, Jim Leyland resigned as manager.

JIM LEYLAND

Jim Leyland has been one of the top managers in baseball for many years, but, through 2010, his only World Series title came with the Marlins in 1997.

Leyland won three straight NL East titles with Pittsburgh from 1990 to 1992. Each of those Pirates teams, though, lost in the NLCS. Leyland took the Detroit Tigers to the World Series as a wild-card team in 2006, but they lost to the St. Louis Cardinals in five games.

In the 1960s, Leyland played six seasons in the Tigers' organization. He then got into coaching in the minor leagues before he reached the big leagues as the Chicago White Sox's third-base coach in 1982. He held that position for four seasons, then became Pittsburgh's manager before the 1986 season.

Through 2010, Leyland was a three-time Manager of the Year. He received the NL honor in 1990 and 1992 and the AL award in 2006.

In January 1999, Huizenga sold the team to John Henry. As Huizenga had done before him, Henry pushed for a new stadium for his team.

On the field, things improved over the next few years. John Boles took over as manager before the 1999 season. He had managed the team for part of the season in 1996 after Rene Lachemann was fired. Under Boles, the Marlins went 64–98 in 1999 and improved to 79–82 in 2000.

The Marlins had some good young players. Outfielder Preston Wilson was the runner-up for NL Rookie of the Year in 1999. In 2000, he hit 31 homers and drove in 121 runs. First baseman Derrek Lee and second baseman Luis Castillo emerged as first-rate infielders. Castillo hit .334 in 2000 and led the majors with 62 stolen bases. Ryan Dempster, Brad Penny,

Musical Owners

The Marlins changed owners twice in a span of three years. The original owner, Wayne Huizenga, sold the team to John Henry in 1999. Three years later, Henry sold the team to Jeffrey Loria, who had previously owned the Montreal Expos. Every owner said the same thing: In order for Florida to have a successful franchise, it needed a new stadium.

and A. J. Burnett all showed that they could be excellent big-league pitchers, and all were younger than 25 years old.

The question was: Did anyone care? After the fire sale, fans felt betrayed and angry. Attendance plummeted. In 2002, when the team improved its record by three wins and finished 79–83, the Marlins averaged just 10,038 fans per home game.

There was, though, at least one positive thing that came out of the 1997 fire sale. Because

Rookie Preston Wilson swings in 1999. Wilson played with Florida through 2002 and helped the team rebound from its disastrous 1998 season.

the Marlins were so bad in 1998, they had the second overall pick in the 1999 amateur draft. The Marlins selected a big, confident high school pitcher from Spring, Texas, named Josh Beckett.

A few years later, Beckett would lead the Marlins back to the top.

CHAPTER 4

BACK ON TOP

The 2003 season began much as the past several had. The Marlins were losing. Fans did not seem to care. On May 10, Florida was in last place in the NL East. The Marlins played most home games in front of small crowds, sometimes fewer than 10,000. That made what happened over the next five months all the more amazing.

The Marlins' turnaround began on May 11, when manager Jeff Torborg was fired and replaced by Jack McKeon. McKeon had managed four times previously in the major leagues, but not since 2000. At age 72, he was old enough to be his players' grandfather.

But he had a magic touch with this team. It helped that some good pitchers who were hurt early in the season became healthy again.

However, it also might have ended up actually helping Florida that those pitchers were hurt. With Josh Beckett,

Shortstop Alex Gonzalez, *right*, catcher Ivan Rodriguez, *middle*, and first baseman Derrek Lee celebrate Florida's 2003 World Series title.

A. J. Burnett, and others injured, the Marlins called up 21-year-old rookie left-hander Dontrelle Willis from the minor leagues in early May.

Willis took the baseball world by storm. He pitched seven shutout innings in the Marlins' 2–0 win over the Oakland Athletics on June 5. Eleven days later, he threw a one-hit shutout as Florida beat the New York Mets 1–0.

"He's something special," center fielder Juan Pierre said after that game. Willis beat the Mets again on June 26 to improve his record to 8–1.

The Marlins hit the ball well that season too. Mike Lowell was a powerhouse. The third baseman led the team with 32 home runs and 105 RBIs. He compiled those statistics despite missing almost all of September with a broken hand. Florida also won with speed. Pierre hit

.305 and led the league with 65 stolen bases. Luis Castillo batted a team-high .314.

By August, Beckett was healthy again. He joined a pitching staff that included Willis, Brad Penny, Mark Redman, and Carl Pavano. Burnett, however, would be limited to four starts the entire season because of an elbow injury.

The Marlins won six straight games in July, then seven straight in September. When Pavano and the Marlins beat the visiting Mets 4–3 on September 26, they clinched the wild-card spot.

With his high leg kick and wicked fastball, rookie pitcher Dontrelle Willis gave the Marlins a big lift in 2003.

Reaching the playoffs, though, was only half of the drama for these magical Marlins. In the NLDS, Florida faced the San Francisco Giants.

The Marlins jumped ahead in the best-of-five NLDS two games to one. They led 7–6 in Game 4 with two outs in the top of the ninth inning. The Giants'

Jack McKeon, shown in May 2003, took over as Marlins manager that month and helped guide the team to a magical season.

Jeffrey Hammonds singled to left field. J. T. Snow, who was on second base, came storming around third, heading home to try to score the tying run.

Left fielder Jeff Conine fielded the ball and fired it to catcher Ivan "Pudge" Rodriguez, who was waiting at home plate. Rodriguez caught the ball and gripped it tightly. Bam! Snow barreled into him in a big collision. But the ball stayed in Rodriguez's glove. Snow was out! The Marlins had won the game and the series on the highlight-reel play.

The Marlins moved on to the NLCS and faced the Chicago Cubs. The Marlins lost three of the first four games of the series. One more defeat and they were done. Beckett responded with a two-hit shut-out in Game 5 as host Florida won 4–0.

Game 6 at Wrigley Field in Chicago will be talked about for years.

Florida was batting in the top of the eighth inning and losing 3–0. With Pierre on second base, Castillo hit a high foul ball down the left-field line. Former Marlin Moises Alou drifted over near the seats and appeared ready to make the catch. As he reached into the seats, a Cubs fan interfered with the ball before Alou could catch it. Foul ball.

Alou was furious. So were Cubs fans. The play rattled the Cubs and re-energized the Marlins. Given a second chance, Castillo walked. After Rodriguez singled, Chicago

THE OLD MAN AND THE SEA

Many 72-year-olds have retired from work. At that age, Jack McKeon decided to take over a last-place baseball team. When he was named manager of the Marlins in May 2003, they were 16–22. Under McKeon, they went 75–49 for the rest of the regular season. He became the oldest manager to win the World Series.

McKeon managed the Marlins for two more seasons, going 83–79 in both 2004 and 2005. He retired with a career record of 1,011–940.

The 2003 Marlins were the only McKeon-managed team that qualified for the playoffs. He had his first managing job with the Kansas City Royals from 1973 to 1975. He then had managing stints with the Oakland Athletics (1977–78), the San Diego Padres (1988–90), and the Cincinnati Reds (1997–2000). From 1981 to 1990, he was general manager of the Padres, helping them reach the World Series in 1984.

shortstop Alex Gonzalez committed an error. The Cubs were falling apart. Derrek Lee drilled a double to tie the score at 3–3. And the hits kept coming. As stunned Cubs fans watched, their team collapsed. Marlins substitute Mike Mordecai added a bases-loaded double.

Florida scored eight runs in the inning and won the game 8–3. It was on to Game 7. As shell-shocked Cubs fans watched, the Marlins won 9–6 to reach the World Series.

In the World Series, the Marlins faced the mighty New York Yankees, who had gone 101–61 in the regular season. Visiting Florida won 3–2 in Game 1 behind Penny. After falling behind two games to one, the Marlins rediscovered their magic. Shortstop Alex Gonzalez, who had been in a slump, hit a home run in the bottom of the 12th inning to give Florida

a 4–3 home victory and tie the Series at two games apiece.

Penny was solid again in Game 5, won 6–4 by host Florida.

In Game 6, McKeon decided that Beckett would be the starting pitcher. Beckett was just 23 years old, but McKeon figured he could handle the pressure of playing in a big World Series game at Yankee Stadium. As usual, McKeon's instincts proved correct. Beckett was sensational. He gave up just five hits and shut out New York as Florida won 2–0. The Marlins were World Series champions again!

"This is indescribable," Castillo said. "How do you find any words for this? . . . Nobody thought we could do this."

The Marlins had fired their manager in May. They had lost one of their best pitchers, Beckett, for nearly two months and

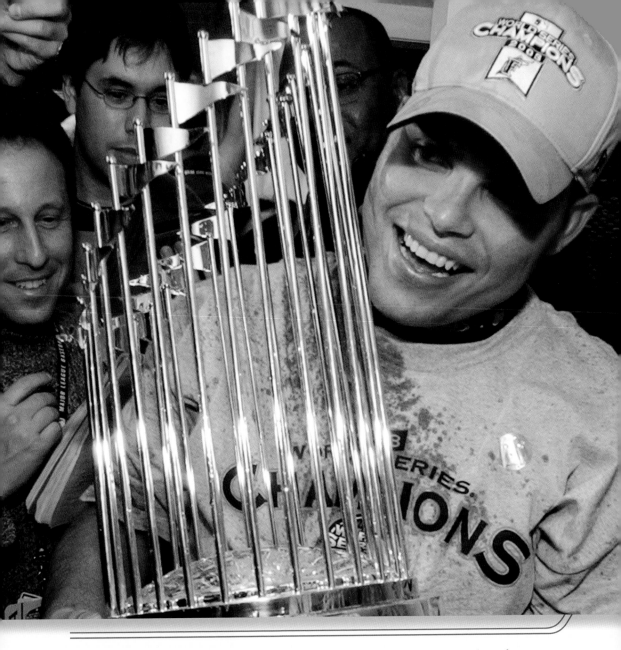

Florida catcher Ivan Rodriguez holds the 2003 World Series trophy after the Marlins upset the Yankees four games to two.

another, Burnett, for almost the entire season. They had lost their top power hitter, Lowell, for most of September. Yet somehow they once again ruled the baseball world.

CHAPTER 5

A BRIGHT FUTURE

As the Marlins and their fans celebrated their improbable 2003 World Series title, many had to wonder: Would there be another fire sale?

At a victory celebration, owner Jeffrey Loria said what Marlins fans wanted to hear: "This is not 1997. This is 2003. We are not dismantling." Not immediately, anyway.

The core of the team returned for 2004. Jack McKeon was back as manager. Pitchers Josh Beckett, Dontrelle Willis, and Carl Pavano returned. So did Juan Pierre, Luis Castillo, Mike Lowell, and "Mr. Marlin," Jeff Conine. Miguel Cabrera, who was a 20-year-old rookie in 2003, blossomed into a star in 2004. He hit .294 with 33 home runs and 112 RBIs.

The Marlins, though, could not recapture the magic of 2003. They finished 83–79 and missed the playoffs.

Shortstop Hanley Ramirez, shown in 2010, has been a consistent star for the Marlins ever since he won the NL Rookie of the Year Award in 2006.

Pitcher Josh Beckett, shown in 2004, was part a talented group of Marlins, but he was traded in a cost-cutting move after the 2005 season.

In 2005, a promising season unraveled quickly in September. Pitcher A. J. Burnett and McKeon did not get along. Cabrera was criticized for poor work habits. The Marlins led the wild-card race on September 12, but they then lost 12 of 15 games. They recovered to finish 83–79, but McKeon stepped down as manager after the season.

At about that time, the stadium issue resurfaced again. Despite winning the World Series twice in a span of seven seasons, the Marlins still were struggling to attract fans. In

2004 and 2005, Florida ranked near the bottom of the NL in attendance.

Loria, the owner, had said he was willing to put a lot of his own money toward a new stadium. He wanted the government to help pay for it, though. The government again refused. Loria was angry. He talked openly of moving the team from South Florida. He said the Marlins would definitely move after the 2010 season if no stadium deal could be reached.

So Loria did what the original Marlins owner, Wayne Huizenga, had done several years earlier. To cut costs, he traded many of the team's highest-paid players. Marlins fans were left to think, *"Not again."*

On November 24, 2005, the Marlins traded Beckett and Lowell, two of their 2003

TRADING PLACES

When Josh Beckett and Mike Lowell were dealt to the Boston Red Sox after the 2005 season, Marlins fans were upset. Two of Florida's biggest stars were being traded for four unknown players.

Beckett and Lowell went on to help the Red Sox win the World Series in 2007. Boston beat the Colorado Rockies four games to none. Lowell was named the World Series MVP.

But the deal proved to be good for the Marlins as well. One of the players the Marlins got in that trade was Hanley Ramirez, who became the 2006 NL Rookie of the Year and the 2009 NL batting champion. Florida also received pitcher Anibal Sanchez, who threw a no-hitter for the Marlins as a rookie in 2006 and finished 10-3 with a 2.83 ERA that season. Sanchez battled injuries the next few seasons but was back pitching well again in 2010.

World Series heroes, to the Boston Red Sox. That same day, they sent slugger Carlos Delgado to the New York Mets. Delgado, a former Toronto Blue Jay, played for Florida for only one season after signing with the team as a free agent. He had 33 homers and 115 RBIs in 2005 for the Marlins. In early December, Florida traded the popular Castillo to the Minnesota Twins and dealt Pierre to the Cubs.

After the trades, the 2006 Marlins had the youngest team and the lowest payroll in the major leagues. That could have been a recipe for disaster all over again. Instead, new manager Joe Girardi led Florida to a 78–84 record. In fact, Girardi would later be named the 2006 NL Manager of the Year. Girardi and Loria had their differences, however, and after one season, Girardi was gone. In his place came Fredi Gonzalez.

Gonzalez was a popular choice to lead the Marlins. Like many in the Miami area, he was a native of Cuba and could speak Spanish and English. He had gone to high school in Miami. He had worked for the Marlins as a minor league coach. It was not a smooth start for Gonzalez, though. The 2007 Marlins lost 91 games.

Then, just as things looked bleak, they turned around again.

One big reason was Hanley Ramirez. The sweet-swinging shortstop from the Dominican

Immediate Success

In 2006, the Marlins accomplished something that had never been done before in the majors. Four rookie pitchers all finished with at least 10 wins: Scott Olsen (12–10), Josh Johnson (12–7), Ricky Nolasco (11–11), and Anibal Sanchez (10–3).

The Marlins' Dan Uggla watches the flight of a home run he hit in 2008. Uggla had more power than typical for a second baseman.

Republic had been acquired from Boston in the Beckett and Lowell trade. By 2008, he was a superstar. He was named the 2006 NL Rookie of the Year after hitting .292 with 17 home runs. He smashed 33 homers in 2008. He won the 2009 NL batting title with a .342 average.

Other additions from the 2005 fire sale also came through. First baseman Mike Jacobs, who came from the Mets, hit 32 homers in 2008. Pitcher Ricky Nolasco, who came from the Cubs, won 15 games.

The Marlins won 84 games in 2008. Second baseman Dan Uggla continued to be a big contributor. He had finished third in the 2006 NL Rookie of the

Marlins president David Samson, *right*, gives pitcher Josh Johnson a tour of the construction site for the team's new ballpark in January 2010.

Year competition won by teammate Ramirez. In 2008, Uggla was named an All-Star and had 32 homers with 92 RBIs.

In 2009, led by Ramirez, Uggla, emerging ace pitcher Josh Johnson, and left fielder Chris Coghlan, who was named NL Rookie of the Year, the Marlins surprised many experts. They had the lowest payroll in the league again, but they were in the playoff chase most of the season. They did not qualify for the postseason but finished 87–75 for their best record since 2003.

By far, though, the biggest news of 2009 came off the field. On March 24, the county government voted to build a new baseball-only stadium for the Marlins in Miami. Finally, the Marlins would have a home of their own. The design included a retractable roof to combat the stormy summer weather.

In 2010, the Marlins did not get off to the start for which they had hoped. With the team's record at 34–36, Florida fired Gonzalez as manager on June 23. His replacement was Edwin Rodriguez, who had been manager of the Marlins' Triple-A affiliate in New Orleans, Louisiana.

For fans who have followed the Marlins during the team's short history, it has been like going on a roller-coaster ride. There have been the highest of highs, with World Series wins in 1997 and 2003. They have been followed by the lowest of lows: the 1997 fire sale, 108 losses in 1998, and another roster purge in 2005.

Now the wild ride appears to be on the way up again.

TIMELINE

1991 — On July 5, major league owners approve the Florida Marlins and the Colorado Rockies as NL expansion teams to begin play in 1993.

1992 — On June 1, the Marlins make catcher Charles Johnson their first-ever pick in the amateur draft.

1993 — The Marlins play their first regular-season game ever on April 5, beating the visiting Los Angeles Dodgers 6–3.

1996 — Florida hires former Pittsburgh Pirates manager Jim Leyland as manager on October 4. The move comes after Rene Lachemann, the first manager in Marlins history, was fired partway through the 1996 season.

1996 — On November 22, the Marlins sign third baseman Bobby Bonilla, a former Pirate. The next month, Florida would sign two more standout players—outfielder Moises Alou, a former Montreal Expo, and pitcher Alex Fernandez, who had played for the Chicago White Sox—as part of an off-season spending spree by owner Wayne Huizenga.

1997 — After defeating the San Francisco Giants in the NLDS and the Atlanta Braves in the NLCS, the Marlins prevail in the World Series over the Cleveland Indians. In Game 7 on October 26, the host Marlins defeat the Indians 3–2 in the 11th inning on a bases-loaded single by Edgar Renteria.

1997 — On November 11, the Marlins trade Alou to the Houston Astros for three minor leaguers. The move is part of an off-season "fire sale" in which Florida deals several expensive veterans, including Alou, outfielder Jeff Conine, and pitcher Kevin Brown, to cut costs.

1998
The Marlins become the first defending World Series champions to lose 100 games. Florida finishes the season 54–108. Leyland resigns as manager after the season.

1999
With the second overall pick in the 1999 amateur draft, the Marlins select high school pitcher Josh Beckett on June 2.

2003
On May 11, with the Marlins in last place at 16–22, Jeff Torborg is fired as manager in his second season in that position. Jack McKeon replaces him.

2003
After beating the Giants in the NLDS, the Marlins rally from a three-games-to-one deficit to defeat the Chicago Cubs in the NLCS. In Game 6 on October 14, the Marlins score eight runs in the eighth inning to win 8–3 at Wrigley Field. The rally is assisted by a Chicago fan who accidentally interfered with a fly ball, preventing the Cubs' left fielder from catching it near the seats.

2003
On October 25, Beckett pitches a five-hit shutout as the Marlins beat the host New York Yankees 2–0 in Game 6 of the World Series to give Florida its second title.

2009
On March 24, Miami-Dade County commissioners approve a new stadium for the Marlins in Miami.

2009
Marlins shortstop Hanley Ramirez becomes the first player in team history to win a batting title. He finishes with a .342 average, 12 points better than the NL runner-up.

QUICK STATS

FRANCHISE HISTORY

1993–

WORLD SERIES
(wins in bold)

1997, 2003

NL CHAMPIONSHIP SERIES

1997, 2003

DIVISION CHAMPIONSHIPS

None

WILD-CARD BERTHS
(1995–)

1997, 2003

KEY PLAYERS
(position[s]; seasons with team)

Josh Beckett (SP; 2001–05)
A. J. Burnett (SP; 1999–2005)
Miguel Cabrera (OF/3B; 2003–07)
Luis Castillo (2B; 1996–2005)
Jeff Conine (LF/1B; 1993–97,
    2003–05)
Charles Johnson (C; 1994–98,
    2001–02)
Juan Pierre (CF; 2003–05)
Hanley Ramirez (SS; 2006–)
Dan Uggla (2B; 2006–)
Dontrelle Willis (SP; 2003–07)

KEY MANAGERS

Jim Leyland (1997–98):
    146–178; 11–5 (postseason)
Jack McKeon (2003–05):
    241–207; 11–6 (postseason)

HOME PARKS

Sun Life Stadium (1993–)
    Previously known as Joe Robbie
    Stadium, Pro Player Park,
    Pro Player Stadium, Dolphins
    Stadium, Dolphin Stadium, and
    Land Shark Stadium

* All statistics through 2010 season

QUOTES AND ANECDOTES

"All I know is it's over and we're on top. . . . This has been a weird series, snow one day, 85 degrees the next. But it had a human element, and that's baseball."
—Florida first baseman Darren Daulton, after the Marlins defeated the Cleveland Indians in seven games in the 1997 World Series

"We shocked the world! We shocked the world!"
—Marlins center fielder Juan Pierre, after Florida beat the New York Yankees 2–0 in Game 6 at Yankee Stadium to win the 2003 World Series

In a span of seven seasons, the Marlins had three players named NL Rookie of the Year: pitcher Dontrelle Willis (2003), shortstop Hanley Ramirez (2006), and left fielder Chris Coghlan (2009).

The Marlins' total team payroll in 2006 was $15 million. The salary of New York Yankees third baseman Alex Rodriguez in 2006 was about $21.6 million.

In 2008, all four of the Marlins' regular starting infielders hit at least 25 home runs. That was the first time in major league history that this happened. Shortstop Hanley Ramirez smacked 33, first baseman Mike Jacobs and second baseman Dan Uggla both hit 32, and third baseman Jorge Cantu belted 29.

GLOSSARY

ace

A team's best starting pitcher.

attendance

The number of fans at a game or the total number of fans attending games in a season.

closer

A relief pitcher who is called on to pitch, usually in the ninth inning, to protect his team's lead.

expansion

In sports, the addition of a franchise or franchises to a league.

finale

The last game of the season.

fire sale

The process when a team trades its high-priced players for cheaper players.

franchise

An entire sports organization, including the players, coaches, and staff.

free agent

A player whose contract has expired and who is able to sign with a team of his choice.

general manager

The executive who is in charge of the team's overall operation. He or she hires and fires managers and coaches, drafts players, and signs free agents.

improbable

Unlikely.

pennant

A flag. In baseball, it symbolizes that a team has won its league championship.

postseason

The games in which the best teams play after the regular-season schedule has been completed.

retractable

Can be opened or closed mechanically depending on the weather.

FOR MORE INFORMATION

Further Reading

Miami Herald. *Florida Marlins: World Series Champions*. Champaign, IL: Sports Publishing, 2004.

Schlossberg, Dan. *Miracle Over Miami: How the 2003 Marlins Shocked the World*. Champaign, IL: Sports Publishing, 2004.

Vecsey, George. *Baseball: A History of America's Favorite Game*. New York: Modern Library, 2008.

Web Links

To learn more about the Florida Marlins, visit ABDO Publishing Company online at **www.abdopublishing.com**. Web sites about the Marlins are featured on our Book Links page. These links are routinely monitored and updated to provide the most current information available.

Places to Visit

National Baseball Hall of Fame and Museum
25 Main Street
Cooperstown, NY 13326
1-888-HALL-OF-FAME
www.baseballhall.org
This hall of fame and museum highlights the greatest players and moments in the history of baseball.

Roger Dean Stadium
4751 Main Street
Jupiter, FL 33458
561-775-1818
www.rogerdeanstadium.com
This has been the Marlins' spring-training ballpark since 2003.

Sun Life Stadium
2267 Dan Marino Boulevard
Miami, FL 33056
305-623-6100
www.sunlifestadium.com
This has been the Marlins' home field since the team's first season in 1993. The Marlins play 81 regular-season games here each year. It will be the team's home stadium through 2011.

INDEX

About the Author

Bo Smolka is a former sports copy editor at the *Baltimore Sun*. He is also a former college sports information director and magazine editor and has won several awards for his writing. His work has appeared in *National Geographic World* and many other national publications. He lives in Baltimore, Maryland, with his wife and two children. When he is not writing, he can often be found coaching his son's baseball teams.

DISCARD